TECHNOLOGY: BLUEPRINTS OF THE FUTURE™

TECHNOLOGY:
BLUEPRINTS OF THE FUTURE™

Aircraft Carriers

Inside and Out

by

Mark Beyer

Illustrations

Leonello Calvetti, Lorenzo Cecchi

The Rosen Publishing Group's
PowerPlus Books™
New York

For the pilots who risk their lives daily to keep freedom alive

Published in 2002 in North America
by The Rosen Publishing Group, Inc., New York

First Edition

Book Design:
Andrea Dué s.r.l. Florence, Italy

Illustrations:
Leonello Calvetti, Lorenzo Cecchi, Luca Massini, Donato Spedaliere

Editor and Photo Researcher:
Joanne Randolph

Associate Editor:
Jason Moring

Library of Congress Cataloging-in-Publication Data

Beyer, Mark (Mark T.)
Aircraft carriers : inside and out / by Mark T. Beyer. — 1st ed.
p. cm. — (Technology—blueprints of the future)
Includes bibliographical references and index.
ISBN 0-8239-6111-7 (library binding)
1. Aircraft carriers—United States—Juvenile literature. [1. Aircraft carriers.]
I. Title. II. Series.
V874.3 .B48 2002
623.8'255—dc21
2001001113
Manufactured in Italy by Eurolitho S.p.A., Milan

Contents

First Line of Defense

Aircraft carriers have been called upon to intervene in world crises more than 200 times since the end of World War II, in 1945. Since that time, when faced with an international crisis, every president's first question has been: "Where are the carriers?" These incredible ships have become the free world's police cars and emergency rescue vehicles. In fact, America and her allies are free, in large part, because of them.

In many ways, these magnificent ships are mirrors of, and even the precursors to, today's age of technology—both in the ship itself and the aircraft that operate from their 4 acre (1.6 ha) flight decks. Civilian nuclear power, including its safety procedures, has many of its origins in navy nuclear power. Similarly, cell phone technology has its origins in the Navy Tactical Data System broadcast network, first installed in the carrier USS *Oriskany* (CVA-34) in 1963. Even the steel these supercarriers are made from, HY-100, requires special high-tech welding procedures. Who knows how this technology might be applied in everyday life?

Despite their five billion dollar price tag, Congress has continued to fund American aircraft carriers, because their technology, and the service they provide, is unequaled in any other nation. For every country, though, aircraft carriers play a vital role as a nation's first line of defense. They are a constant presence that can be mobilized quickly and effectively in combat or relief-providing missions.

What does all this mean to you? Besides learning about the exciting technical capabilities that make aircraft carriers and their airwing so effective, you could be in the position of improving the operation of carriers and aircraft at sea someday. Or, maybe you will, through studying these exciting machines, think of some way to apply their technology to improve everyday life for everyone. The future of naval aviation and aircraft carriers is as large and exciting as the floating cities that are already out there patrolling the ocean—and you could be a part of it.

I hope that you find it as exciting as I did in my thirty years at sea in America's great navy.

Pete Clayton
Commander, U.S. Navy (retired)
Chief Engineer, USS *Ranger* (CV-61) during the Gulf War

Right: This is the deck of the aircraft carrier *Ticonderoga*. Notice the planes and the helicopter on the deck. This carrier is waiting for the *Apollo 17* space capsule landing in 1972.

Below: An F-14 Tomcat is being directed to the catapults by the flight crew. From the steam it appears another plane has just taken off.

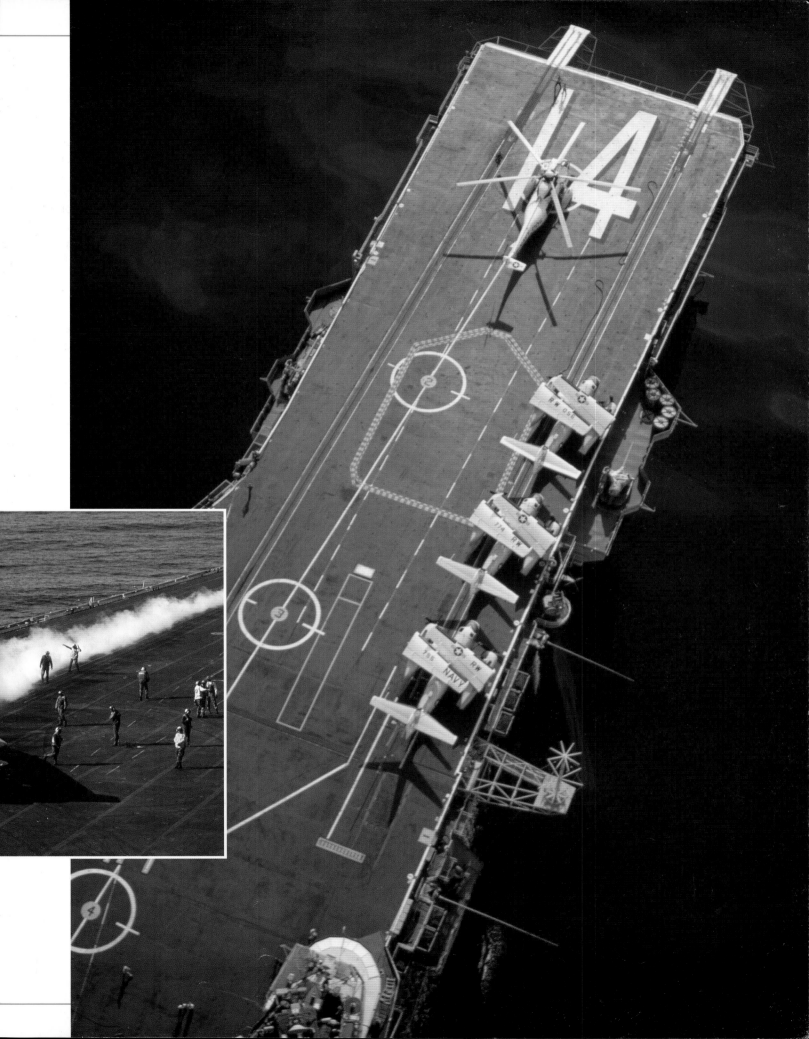

Why the Aircraft Carrier Was Built

In 1903, Wilbur and Orville Wright flew the first airplane. This airplane had two wings and two engines, but no wheels. It landed on metal runners, like those on a snow sled. The Wright brothers' plane amazed people. Suddenly people wanted to learn how to fly airplanes, but planes cost a lot of money to build.

By 1908, only wealthy people and stunt pilots flew airplanes. Airplanes, however, could not be flown safely in bad weather. They could not be flown at night, either. Many pilots crashed and died in the early years of airplanes. For these reasons, the U.S. military did not think airplanes could be used as weapons. Later that year, a stunt pilot helped to change their minds.

Glenn Curtiss was an aviation pioneer. He built his own planes and flew stunts for paying crowds. In 1908, he built a model of a navy battleship on the ground. He flew his plane in simulated bombing runs. The U.S. Navy heard about Curtiss's flight. The Navy liked Curtiss's idea, but they were not convinced that a plane could be useful in battle.

A few years later, the Navy learned that the Germans tried to fly a plane off a ship. To see whether this could be done successfully, the Navy hired civilian pilot Eugene Ely to try the stunt. In November 1910, Eugene Ely flew his Curtiss biplane off the deck of the USS *Birmingham*. Two months later, he attempted to land his plane on the ship's deck, in San Francisco Bay. Ely's plane dropped a hook from its back. Twelve arrester cables stretched across the deck to catch the hook as the plane landed. Ely missed the first eleven cables. The hook snagged the twelfth cable and stopped the plane on the platform.

The *Birmingham* was not originally designed for airplane use. It had a 100-foot (30.5-m) wood platform specially built on its deck so the plane could take off and land. The Navy decided they needed to design a ship that could be used as a floating airport.

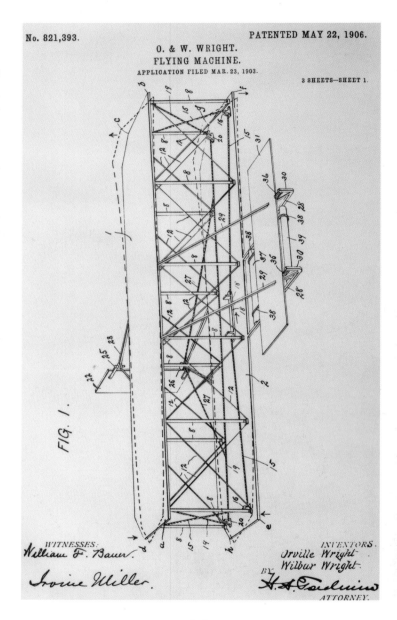

Above: When the Wright Brothers drew this sketch for their first patent application, they never realized how dramatically it would reshape the world. This was the crate they built in 1906.

Top (illustration): The *Flyer* designed by Wilbur and Orville Wright

Middle: Eugene Ely lands his small biplane on the deck of the USS *Pennsylvania*. He made the first successful shipboard aircraft launch from the USS *Birmingham* a year earlier.

Right: Glenn Curtiss, pioneer aviator, is shown here in a *Curtiss Condor*. He revolutionized the way the navy fought and changed the face of aviation in general.

The First Carriers

Naval aviation began slowly. During World War I, many countries worked on building some kind of aircraft carrier. The first carriers did not fly planes off their decks. They used navy cruisers, battleships, and destroyers to carry seaplanes. The seaplanes were let down into the water using cranes. Seaplanes took off from the water and were used for battle and to spot enemy ships.

Below: A Douglas A-4 Skyhawk attack fighter launches off the deck of an aircraft carrier.

The British used their seaplanes to fight German ships. The U.S. Navy used its planes to spot the enemy. These planes did not have guns or bombs. When the pilot spotted the enemy, he flew back to his ship. Once on board, the pilot gave the enemy's position. Only then were naval guns used to fire at targets.

Soon, though, the British built decks on the tops of tow barges. Tow barges were flat ships, so no major rebuilding had to be done. Flight decks were laid on the barges, and the British began launching wheeled fighter airplanes off these decks. These fighter planes attacked German airfields and zeppelins, or helium-filled blimps. The British had great success with these barges, and they soon built carrier platforms atop the hulls of other ships. By the end of the war, the aircraft carrier was the ship wanted by the navies of every country.

All planes need the wind's help to fly. As a plane moves fast down a runway, the shape of the wings forces the air to flow over the top of the wings. As air presses over the top of the wings, the air below the wings becomes lighter. At the right speed, this kind of airflow allows the plane to lift off the ground and fly. A light plane can lift off at much slower speeds than can a heavy plane. Airplanes that were used in World War I lifted off the ground at about 50 miles per hour (80.5 km/h). Today's heavier jets must go at least 150 miles per hour (241.4 km/h) to lift off the ground.

Below: This is a longitudinal section through the USS *Yorktown* CV 5, built at Newport News Shipyard, Virginia, and completed in 1937. Its open-type hangar could hold 80 aircraft.

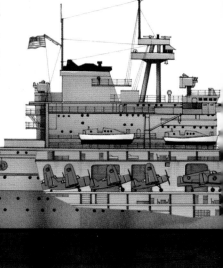

Runways on the ground can be made any length to let airplanes pick up enough speed to fly. However, on a ship the amount of space is limited. Early aircraft carriers were converted armored cruisers with no more than 100-foot (30.5-m) long platforms built on the bow, or front of the ship. To help the airplane get lift, the carriers cruised into the wind at high speeds. An early aircraft carrier could travel 25 miles per hour (40.2 km/h). This was about as fast as any navy ship on the water. These combined forces helped early aircraft lift off from carriers and fly into battle. Still there were times when planes ran off the front edges of the ships' platforms and crashed into the sea. Often, as many planes were damaged landing or taking off as were shot down in battle.

In 1915, the U.S. Navy invented a catapult to help planes gather enough speed to take off from the platform. These first catapults were made of springs. The plane sat on a deck that sloped downward toward the water, like a slide. The catapult was attached to the plane's wheel axle. The spring pushed the plane quickly down the ramp. This speed allowed the plane to use the wind to pick up its wings and let the engine gain power. Once in the air and under its own engine power, the plane could safely fly.

After World War I, for the first time some U.S. ships were specifically designed to carry and to fly planes. They were made with long decks used as runways. Airplanes flew off the ship's bow and landed on its stern. These new aircraft carriers had huge engines that made them the fastest ships in the Navy. Hangars held more than eighty planes, all ready to take off at the first sign of the enemy. Carriers soon became the most powerful ships on the water.

Above: A Sopwith Strutter takes off from a platform over the twin barrels of a 12-inch (305 mm) gun turret.

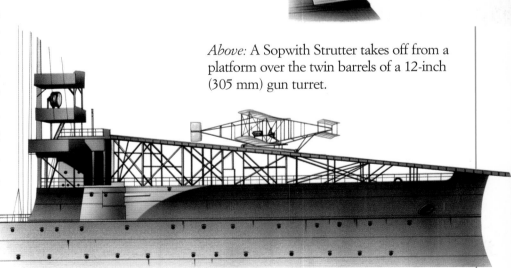

Above: Eugene Ely's Curtiss Pusher rolls down the ramp of the scout cruiser USS *Birmingham* in November 1910.

The USS *Langley, Saratoga* and *Lexington*

The U.S. Navy built its first aircraft carrier in 1919. It converted the supply ship USS *Jupiter* into a flat-topped aircraft carrier and renamed it the *Langley*. The *Langley* was never used in battle, but for twenty years, the U.S. Navy used the *Langley* for carrier training. The first naval aviators learned to take off and to land on the *Langley's* 300-foot (91-m) deck. The navy learned more about using a carrier's speed to build wind for a plane's takeoff. Their engineers also developed a better catapult. Aircraft carriers would need all this new information and technology. Airplanes were becoming larger, faster, and heavier. New carriers were needed to use these faster, heavier, and deadlier planes.

New carriers would need to be longer, taller, and wider than any ship in the fleet. Planes needed longer decks to take off and land. Hangar decks needed to be sufficiently tall and wide to hold dozens of planes. The flight deck had to have space for airplane elevators and storage. Larger engines were needed to allow these huge ships to move fast in the water. All of these needs made carrier designers important people in the 1920s. They began designing what would be the largest ships ever built.

In the 1920s, the British, the French, and the Japanese navies all were building big carriers. The U.S. Navy had two partly-built battle cruisers. They were named the USS *Saratoga* and the USS *Lexington*. Their hulls were the only parts that had been built. The Navy decided to convert these ships into aircraft carriers.

Both ships were commissioned, or put to use, in 1927. They were the largest carriers in the world. They both weighed 36,000 tons (32,658.7 t). Four engines turned four huge propellers that steamed the ships up to 35 knots, or more than 40 miles per hour (64.4 km/h). Speed helped the carriers to get into battle quickly and to get planes into the air faster than any carrier on the ocean. Each carrier held ninety airplanes. This was more than twice the number of planes held by either the Japanese or the British carriers.

Their designs were different from other carriers, too. The *Saratoga* and the *Lexington* each had a bridge, or control tower, set off to the starboard, or right, side of the ship. These "islands" sat in the middle of the ship so flight operations on both ends of the ship were visible.

Below (top and middle): The *Saratoga* was commissioned in 1927. She was one of three prewar U.S. carriers to survive World War II. After the devastating damage inflicted by the surprise Japanese attack at Pearl Harbor, she was the backbone of the U.S. defenses and flew thousands of airstrikes. She was struck by torpedoes, bombs, and Kamikaze planes and had to be repaired. In 1944, she was refitted with better antiaircraft guns. After the war, she was sunk during the atomic bomb tests at Bikini Atoll in 1946.

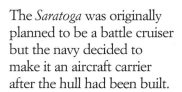

The *Saratoga* was originally planned to be a battle cruiser but the navy decided to make it an aircraft carrier after the hull had been built.

They also had open hangars below the flight deck. Huge doors opened on the sides of the hangar deck. Open hangers allowed the greatest airflow through the hangar, sweeping away exhaust and gasoline fumes. In rain or rough seas, the huge doors close to protect people and aircraft.

Finally, three elevators were used to bring up planes from the hangar deck. Once on the flight deck, the planes could be quickly wheeled to a catapult and launched into the air. When planes landed, they were wheeled to an elevator and were taken below so that the landing area was clear for the next plane. These designs helped the carrier crews work efficiently. Fast service meant getting the planes back into the air. The *Saratoga* and the *Lexington* were the first modern carriers. All future U.S. Navy aircraft carriers would look much like these two ships.

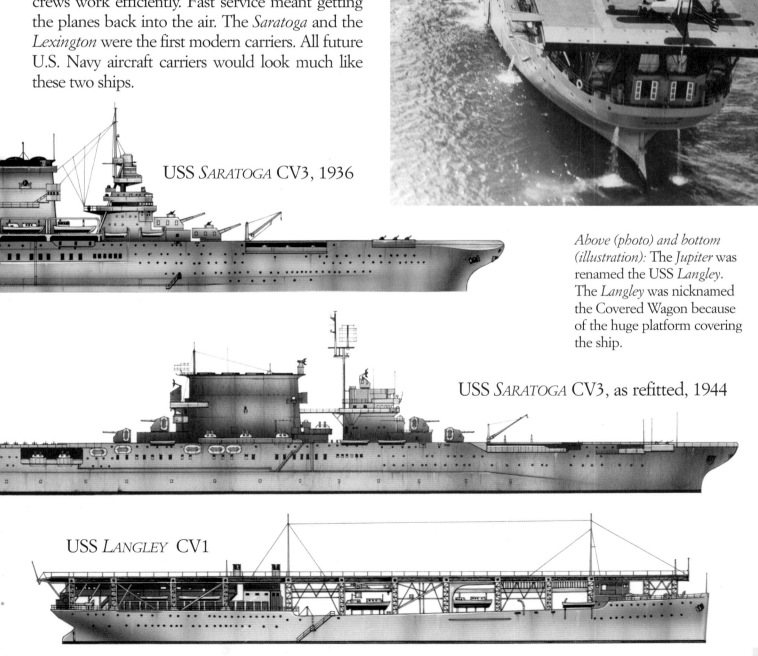

USS *SARATOGA* CV3, 1936

Above (photo) and bottom (illustration): The *Jupiter* was renamed the USS *Langley*. The *Langley* was nicknamed the Covered Wagon because of the huge platform covering the ship.

USS *SARATOGA* CV3, as refitted, 1944

USS *LANGLEY* CV1

The Battle of Midway

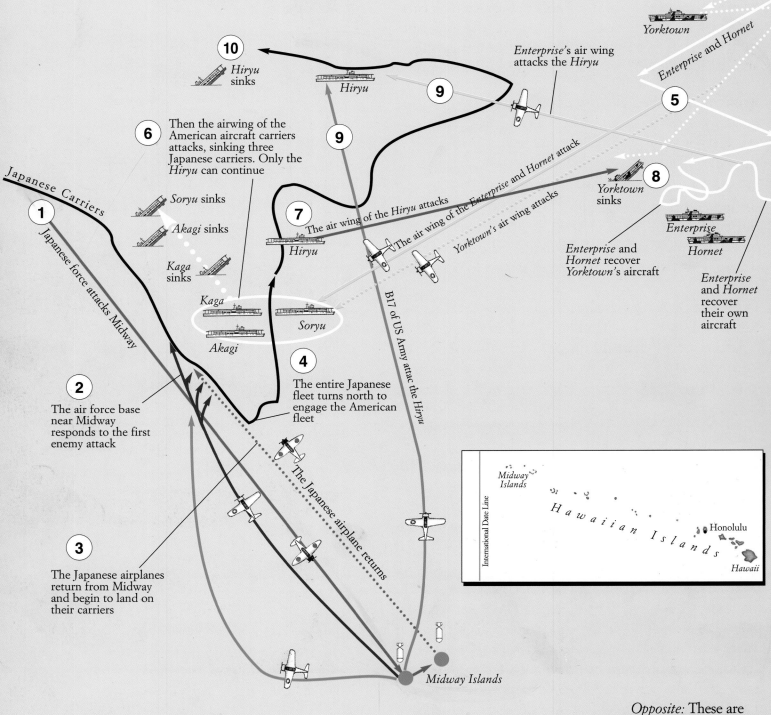

10 *Hiryu* sinks

6 Then the airwing of the American aircraft carriers attacks, sinking three Japanese carriers. Only the *Hiryu* can continue

Soryu sinks

Akagi sinks

Kaga sinks

Kaga

Akagi

Soryu

4 The entire Japanese fleet turns north to engage the American fleet

7

Hiryu

The air wing of the *Hiryu* attacks

9

Hiryu

9

Enterprise's air wing attacks the *Hiryu*

The air wing of the *Enterprise* and *Hornet* attack

Yorktown's air wing attacks

B17 of US Army attac the Hiryu

5

Yorktown

Enterprise and *Hornet*

8 *Yorktown* sinks

Enterprise

Hornet

Enterprise and *Hornet* recover *Yorktown's* aircraft

Enterprise and *Hornet* recover their own aircraft

1 Japanese Carriers

Japanese force attacks Midway

2 The air force base near Midway responds to the first enemy attack

3 The Japanese airplanes return from Midway and begin to land on their carriers

The Japanese airplane returns

Midway Islands

Midway Islands

International Date Line

Hawaiian Islands

Honolulu

Hawaii

Opposite: These are some of the planes that were used in the Battle of Midway by the United States and the Japanese.

World War II (1939–1945) proved that aircraft carriers were the most powerful ships on the ocean. A carrier's power comes not from the guns on the ship, but from the planes that are launched to fight enemy ships and carriers. A carrier's speed is its next best weapon.

Aircraft carriers are forward-presence ships. They must be able to get to a battle quickly. Carriers get close enough to launch their airplanes, but not close enough for enemy ships to easily find and attack them. During World War II, carrier planes could fly almost six hours before they needed refueling. This meant carriers could be about 300 miles (482.8 km) from a battle. Its planes flew to the battle, dropped their bombs, and returned to the carrier as fast as possible.

The Battle of Midway is the most famous carrier naval battle of World War II. The U.S. Navy broke the Japanese secret code and found out that a huge naval force was on its way to capture the Midway Island, more than a 1,000 miles (1,609.3 km) north of Pearl Harbor, Hawaii. If the Japanese captured Midway, they would cut off an important U.S. supply point.

The U.S. sent a battle group to fight the Japanese. It included the carriers USS *Yorktown*, USS *Hornet*, and USS *Enterprise*. On June 6, 1942, these aircraft carriers sent out torpedo and bomber planes to find the Japanese battle group. After hours of searching, the planes spotted four Japanese carriers and many destroyers. The torpedo and bomber planes attacked the carriers. At the end of a long battle that lasted for most of the day, all four of the Japanese carriers were sunk. The USS *Yorktown* was also sunk. These four Japanese carriers were the strength of the Japanese navy, and Japan never recovered from the loss. Sinking them helped the United States to defeat the Japanese three years later. This battle was important for another reason: It was the first naval battle fought in which none of the enemy ships ever got sight of each other. Airplanes did all the fighting. The U.S. Navy discovered that aircraft carriers were the ships of the future.

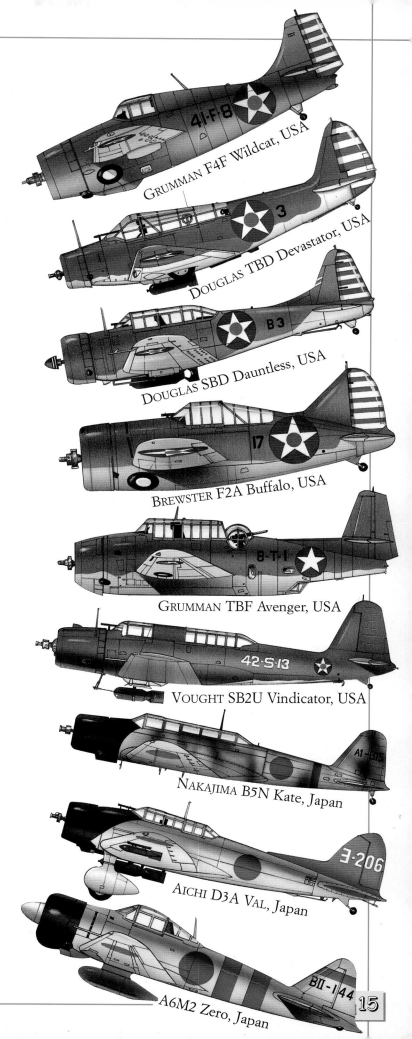

GRUMMAN F4F Wildcat, USA

DOUGLAS TBD Devastator, USA

DOUGLAS SBD Dauntless, USA

BREWSTER F2A Buffalo, USA

GRUMMAN TBF Avenger, USA

VOUGHT SB2U Vindicator, USA

NAKAJIMA B5N Kate, Japan

AICHI D3A VAL, Japan

A6M2 Zero, Japan

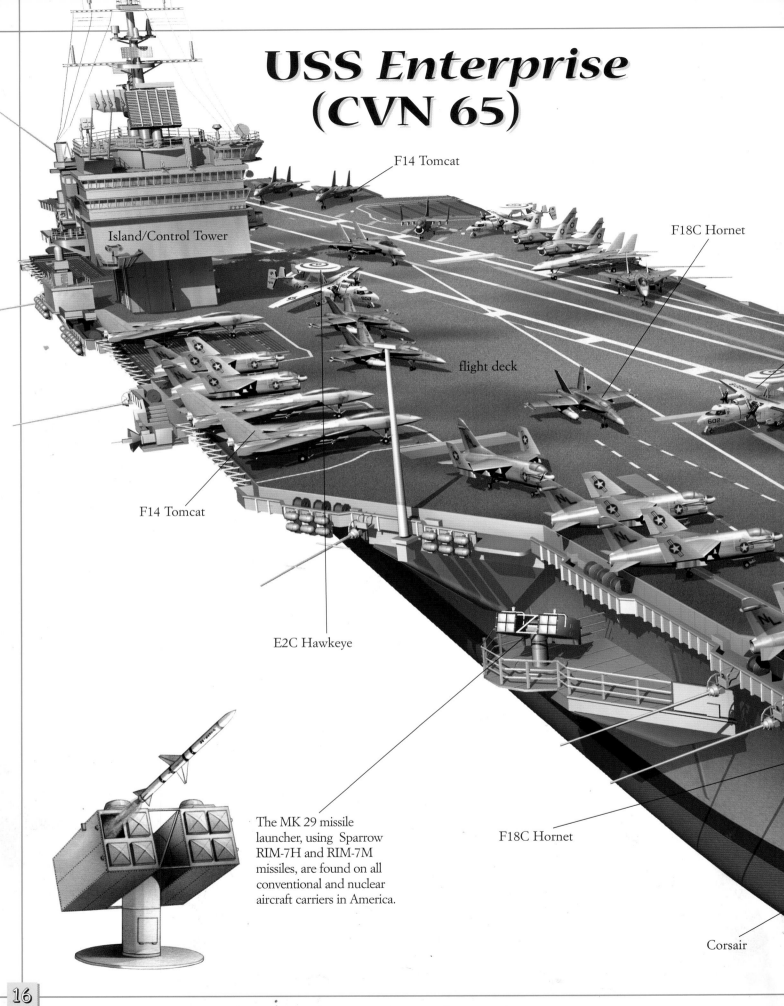

USS Enterprise (CVN 65)

F14 Tomcat

F18C Hornet

Island/Control Tower

flight deck

F14 Tomcat

E2C Hawkeye

The MK 29 missile launcher, using Sparrow RIM-7H and RIM-7M missiles, are found on all conventional and nuclear aircraft carriers in America.

F18C Hornet

Corsair

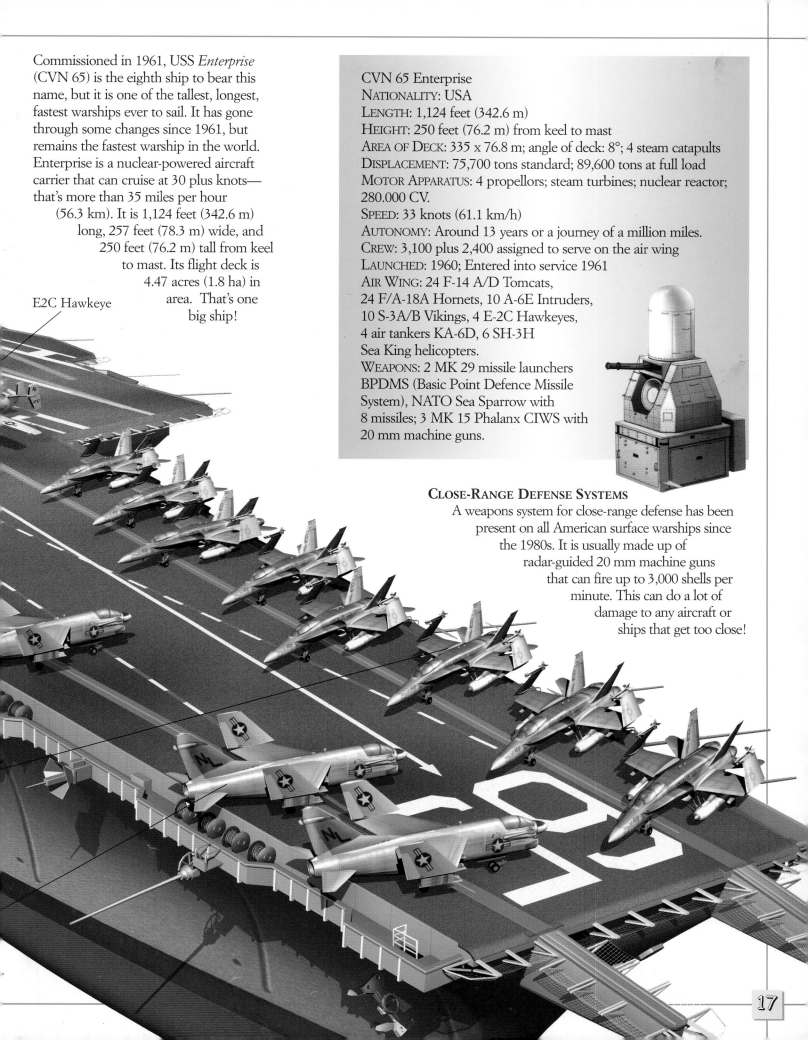

Commissioned in 1961, USS *Enterprise* (CVN 65) is the eighth ship to bear this name, but it is one of the tallest, longest, fastest warships ever to sail. It has gone through some changes since 1961, but remains the fastest warship in the world. Enterprise is a nuclear-powered aircraft carrier that can cruise at 30 plus knots—that's more than 35 miles per hour (56.3 km). It is 1,124 feet (342.6 m) long, 257 feet (78.3 m) wide, and 250 feet (76.2 m) tall from keel to mast. Its flight deck is 4.47 acres (1.8 ha) in area. That's one big ship!

E2C Hawkeye

CVN 65 Enterprise
NATIONALITY: USA
LENGTH: 1,124 feet (342.6 m)
HEIGHT: 250 feet (76.2 m) from keel to mast
AREA OF DECK: 335 x 76.8 m; angle of deck: 8°; 4 steam catapults
DISPLACEMENT: 75,700 tons standard; 89,600 tons at full load
MOTOR APPARATUS: 4 propellors; steam turbines; nuclear reactor; 280.000 CV.
SPEED: 33 knots (61.1 km/h)
AUTONOMY: Around 13 years or a journey of a million miles.
CREW: 3,100 plus 2,400 assigned to serve on the air wing
LAUNCHED: 1960; Entered into service 1961
AIR WING: 24 F-14 A/D Tomcats, 24 F/A-18A Hornets, 10 A-6E Intruders, 10 S-3A/B Vikings, 4 E-2C Hawkeyes, 4 air tankers KA-6D, 6 SH-3H Sea King helicopters.
WEAPONS: 2 MK 29 missile launchers BPDMS (Basic Point Defence Missile System), NATO Sea Sparrow with 8 missiles; 3 MK 15 Phalanx CIWS with 20 mm machine guns.

CLOSE-RANGE DEFENSE SYSTEMS

A weapons system for close-range defense has been present on all American surface warships since the 1980s. It is usually made up of radar-guided 20 mm machine guns that can fire up to 3,000 shells per minute. This can do a lot of damage to any aircraft or ships that get too close!

The Supercarrier

In the 1950s, jet planes came into use, meaning modern aircraft carriers had to be redesigned. Jets were heavier, landed at much faster speeds, and used more fuel than the propeller planes of World War I or II. Jets also used larger bombs and could get back and forth to a battle quicker. This meant carriers had to be larger to store more bombs and fuel, so jets could be used repeatedly in the same battle. Finally, carriers designed after World War II had to be able to stay at sea for months at a time. By the 1970s, the U.S. Navy needed a supercarrier.

THE DESIGN FITS THE NEED

Designing the first supercarrier took a lot of planning. There were already different kinds of carriers. Attack carriers brought jet planes quickly to a battle zone. Helicopter carriers and light carriers (see page 38) brought assault helicopters, smaller jets, and troops to a battle.

The Navy wanted to modify the attack carrier. They wanted to build an attack carrier that was the most powerful ship on the sea. They decided to build a ship that was a floating city. There would be more than six thousand people working on the ship in hundreds of different jobs. The ship needed a hospital, living quarters, kitchens, freezers, and a post office. It also needed workshops, fuel storage tanks, and an airplane hangar for more than eighty-five aircraft. Above all, it needed the best naval aviation technology available.

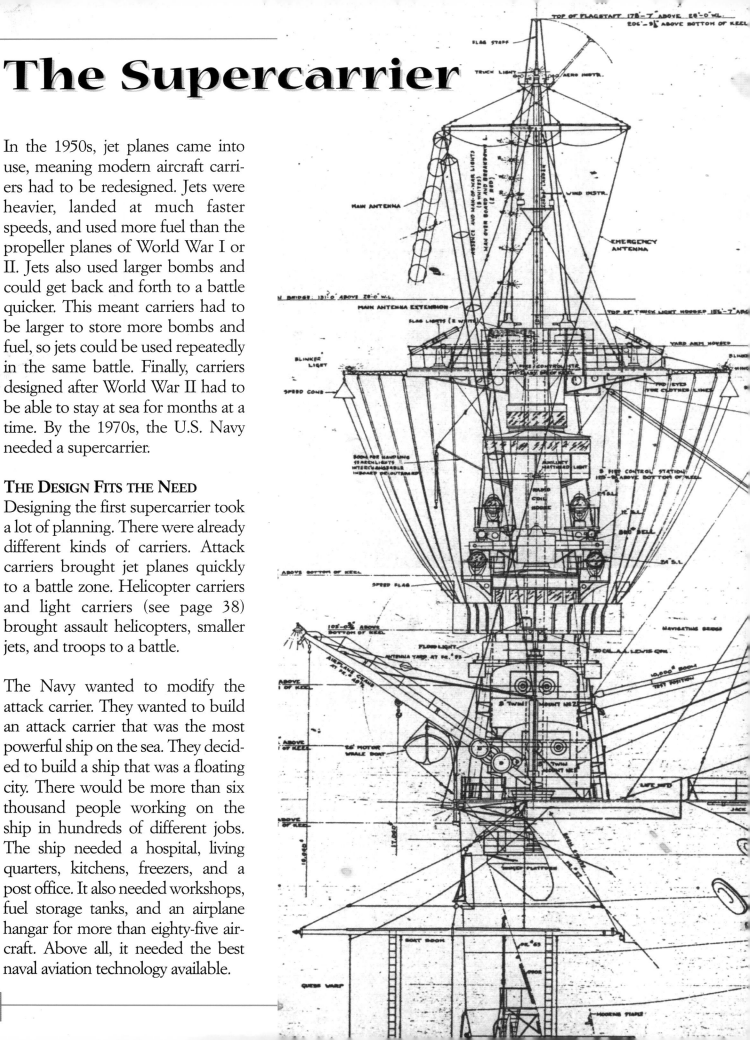

Right: This is an aerial view of the Newport News shipyard. An aircraft carrier cannot be larger than the place used to build it. The Newport News Shipbuilding yard in Virginia is the only place where aircraft carriers are built. The yard's biggest building area is Dry Dock 12. It is more than 2,200 feet (670.6 m) long and five stories deep.

Finally, it needed two nuclear reactors that were safer than any other nuclear reactor on Earth. The designers went to work.

More than twenty years later, eleven supercarriers are at sea. The USS *Harry S. Truman* is the newest carrier. It was commissioned in 1998. The twelfth carrier, the USS *Ronald Reagan*, will not be completed until around 2003. These new carriers cost more than four billion dollars apiece. Let's see how they were built.

Left (photo): The hull of the USS *Ronald Reagan* is being placed.

Left (blueprint): This is what an aircraft carrier blueprint looks like. All the blueprints needed for just one carrier could fill a small building!

19

Designing a Supercarrier

Aircraft carriers are designed with the help of computers. Computer Aided Design (CAD) programs help designers see each part made that connects a ship. Hundreds of engineers help design an aircraft carrier. They make thousands of drawings. Each design and drawing goes through many drafts before a blueprint is made.

There are thousands of parts that make up a complete ship. All parts must fit together exactly. Computers help designers "see" parts of a ship before drawing blueprints. They can design where wires and pipes will travel throughout the ship. Designers can look at whole sections of a ship to see how each section will connect with the section next to it. Designers also can see how certain parts of the ship operate. For instance, steam-powered catapults sit beneath the surface of the flight deck. Their parts move hundreds of times every day. Designers can use their computers to see how a catapult will work before sending it to be made. Designers also can see how protective blast plates, using hydraulic power, move up and away from the flight deck. They want to be sure that the plates will be able to effectively do their job of protecting people from jet blasts. Using computers, the designers can also see how much room is needed for both the catapult systems and the blast plates. All of these parts must be understood long before a ship is put together. This kind of design technology prevents many mistakes that would cost more money and much more time to fix.

A MEETING OF THE MINDS: THE PEOPLE BEHIND BUILDING A SUPERCARRIER
The U.S. Navy begins thinking about building a new ship when an old ship becomes unusable. The Kitty Hawk-class carriers were built in the 1950s. By the 1970s, these carriers were outdated. Oil-burning furnaces powered the Kitty Hawk-class carriers but the Navy needed nuclear powered carriers so that refueling would be unnecessary. Also, Kitty Hawk-class carriers were too small to handle the faster, heavier jets being used. It was time for a new nuclear-powered supercarrier.

The U.S. Navy plans ten years ahead for the design and the building of a new carrier. The first five years are used to raise funds and to design the ship. Admirals, or Navy leaders, first ask Congress for the more than four billion dollars needed to build modern aircraft carriers. Congress listens to what the naval experts need. The two groups talk about technology and the money needed to pay for it. When Congress understands what all of that money will be used for, they set aside money for building the ship. Not all the money is

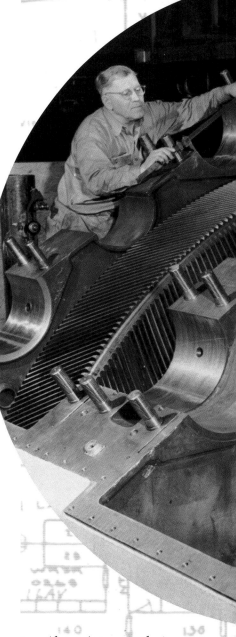

Above: A man works in the engine room of the USS *Saratoga.* The propulsion equipment was made by General Electric Company's Medium Steam Turbine Generator and Gear Department.

Right: A broken propeller blade is seen on the French nuclear aircraft carrier *Charles de Gaulle.* The carrier was on sea trials in the Atlantic Ocean when a blade section split from the propeller.

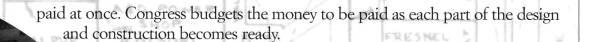

paid at once. Congress budgets the money to be paid as each part of the design and construction becomes ready.

Sometimes technology changes even as the ship is being built. Naval experts work with designers throughout the building phase. Most new technologies can be fitted into the supercarrier designs with few changes. For example, if a new defensive missile system becomes available, it must be worked into the design. Designers look for places in the drawings where changes can be made without interrupting building. Maybe a lifeboat system, that has not yet been built, can be moved 20 feet (7.6 meters) to allow space for the missiles.

The power plant of a Nimitz-class supercarrier is special. Its two nuclear reactors allow the ship to stay at sea for more than twenty years without refueling. Now that is staying power! In order for nuclear power to be a real option, though, the Navy had to make sure the reactors were safe. Radioactive steam made by the reactor to run the engines can kill people. The heat created by the reactors needed to be monitored by electronic machines. A nuclear reactor that got too hot could melt through the steel ship, or worse, explode. Specially-trained technicians monitor fuel rod use and replacement with the help of electronic machines. The Navy knew that any nuclear accident would mean the end of a nuclear-powered navy.

Therefore, design and construction of every nuclear power plant is very detailed. Each step of its design and construction undergoes tough inspection. For example, hundreds of welded pipes used in a nuclear reactor must be x-rayed for cracks. Regular inspections continue for the life of the reactor.

THE NUCLEAR POWER PLANT

All power to a carrier comes from its two nuclear reactors. Nuclear power works through heat and steam. The heat given off by the nuclear reactors boils water into steam. The steam is then sent through pipes that turn four turbines. Turbines are huge magnets that spin around huge wheels made of copper cables. This spinning action creates electricity.

An aircraft carrier uses a huge amount of electricity. After all, this is a floating city. Almost every piece of equipment used on a carrier needs electricity to work. Many of the decks sit below the water. Lights must be on at all times down on these decks. Machine shops repairing airplanes use electricity. The ovens that make bread for sailors to eat use electricity. A supercarrier's nuclear power plant has the ability to produce enough electricity to keep a city of 90,000 people working around the clock.

Building the Supercarrier

All of the biggest Navy ships are built at the Newport News Shipbuilding yard in Newport News, Virginia. This shipbuilding yard has been around for more than one hundred years. The yard uses huge cranes and dry docks along the James River to build ships. Thousands of workers help build these big ships, each working on the same ship for many years.

Aircraft carriers are the biggest ships in the world, and building one requires a lot of space. Dry docks help builders put together a carrier before it goes into the water. A dry dock keeps the water out until the hull has been built. Then it is flooded and the ship can float. There is a problem, though. The largest dry dock can only hold only 33 feet (10 m) of water. A carrier hull sits with more than 30 feet (9.1 m) of its hull under the water, called the ship's draft, when it is completed and loaded with planes, crew, and supplies. That means the entire ship cannot be completed in dry dock. The dry dock is used just to finish the hull. Once the hull is built, the ship is floated out of the dock and brought to a deep-water pier on the James River. Here the carrier is completed.

Dry Dock 12 is the place where all deep-draft ships are built. Dry Dock 12 is more than 2,000 feet (609.6 m) long. That's twice as long as the carrier will be when it is completed. Dry Dock 12 is more than five stories deep. That's enough space to safely put together the hull. The bottom of the dock is thick cement. This floor must be able to take the weight of a ship without cracking or sinking.

A huge bridge crane sits on steel wheels above the dock. It moves from one end to the other on steel tracks. This crane is able to lift up to 900 tons (816.5 t). It is used to lift the hundreds of huge steel sections that fit together to complete the carrier.

Behind Dry Dock 12 are machine shops that are used to build many of the smaller parts of the ship. Heating and air-conditioning ducts must be made to fit throughout the ship.

Right: This is a drawing of the dry dock at Newport News Shipyard, in Virginia. Wooden blocks have been laid in the bottom to protect the ship as it is being built.

Below: The *Ronald Reagan* is being constructed at Newport News Shipyard.

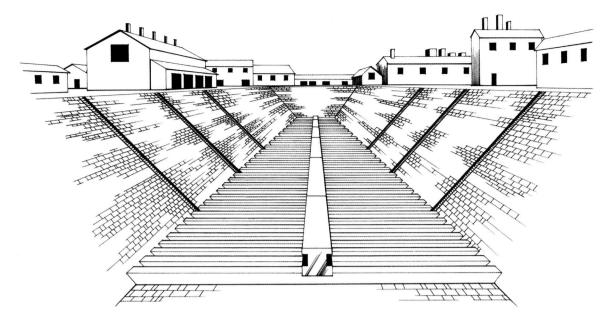

Bulkheads, or walls between every room in the ship, must be made to fit exactly in the space designed for them. Wide pipes used for ventilation must also be cut and welded before being fitted into the carrier.

The thousands of workers who help to build a carrier each have a special job. Hundreds of electricians run wire through pipes to connect all the electronics throughout the ship. They also connect the many thousands of light switches and light fixtures. Welders put together each piece of metal that connects floors, walls, doorways, ceilings, and even tables. Plumbers connect pipes, showers, and faucets. As these armies of builders complete one part of the ship, they move to another until all parts required in the blueprint designs are completed.

Right: These drawings show the scale of an aircraft carrier. A modern carrier is as long as the Empire State Building is tall!

THE EMPIRE STATE BUILDING

USS *JOHN F. KENNEDY*, 1975

Construction Begins

The aircraft carrier USS *Ronald Reagan* CVN 76 under construction at Newport News Shipbuilding for the U.S. Navy.

A completed carrier weighs more than 95,000 tons (86,183 t). At least two-thirds of that weight comes from the steel used for the hull, the control tower, and all the internal compartments.

LAYING THE BUILDING BLOCKS

Building the Navy's newest ships begins with the oldest technology. Hundreds of huge wooden blocks are placed on the floor of Dry Dock 12. The ship's hull will sit on these blocks for the next few years. Some of these blocks are larger than a car. Wood blocks are used, because they can support a lot of weight while cushioning the steel that sits on top. Cushioning the steel hull guards it from cracking as more weight is added during building.

LAYING THE KEEL

Building an aircraft carrier starts with the keel. The keel, or bottom of the ship, is built in sections and is brought to the shipyard. Huge cranes lift the first section of the keel from the dock. They place it onto the blocks on the dry dock floor.

As each keel section is placed, shipbuilders weld it together. A new section of the keel is not placed until the last section is complete. This job is the most important part of the process. The ship's keel must be put together exactly as the blueprints demand. Otherwise the ship will not float or sail correctly. This work takes up to five months. Laying the keel is so important that a ceremony is held when the job is done!

PUTTING THE PIECES TOGETHER

Other work goes on while the keel is being built. Bulkheads and compartments are made and set aside until it is time to put them in place. They are made in advance so that construction does not come to a stop while the part is being made. When the compartments are needed, a work crew or a crane simply picks them up and places them where they should go in the ship.

Not all the parts of the ship are made at the same time, though. There are simply too many walls, doors, stairways, and floors— no shipyard wants all of these parts laying around for months! Some parts of a ship are made by manufacturers on a "ready to use" timetable. Shipbuilders call a manufacturer near the time they need a certain section. The manufacturer then builds it and sends it to the shipyard. By the time the shipyard receives the section, they are ready to put it together with the rest of the ship. This method saves time, space, and money.

Finding Your Way Around a Carrier

Miles (km) of passageways snake through a carrier. Maps are placed in each compartment to show people where they are. A carrier is divided into 256 frames. Frame one is at the bow, and frame 256 is at the stern. Passageway numbers are divided into even and odd numbers. Even-numbered passageways are on the left side of the ship. Odd-numbered passageways are on the right side of the ship.

COMPARTMENTS, PIPES, CABLES, AND WIRES

As the floors of the carrier are laid, so are the compartments, the pipes, the cables, and the wires. There are more than one thousand compartments on a carrier. Each compartment has wires, pipes, and cables coming into it. The pipes, wires, and cables of a ship act like your body's veins. They help the ship live by carrying electricity, air, and water to all parts of the ship. Shipbuilders rely on the blueprints to tell them where each pipe, cable, and wire must go. More than 900 miles (1,448.4 m) of pipes, cables, and wires run throughout a carrier. There are also 30,000 light fixtures. Shipbuilders begin laying these pipes, cables, and wires as soon as the lowest deck is laid.

LAUNCHING THE SUPERCARRIER

A carrier sits in dry dock for up to three years. It sits at a deep-water pier for the next two years. The ship is ready to sail when all the computers, the pumps, the beds, the tables, and the toilets are finally in place. Before joining the U.S. Navy for duty, however, a carrier sails out for sea trials. Sea trials test every part of the ship. Sailors use every piece of equipment and test every moving part. Trials take months to complete.

On the flight deck, the steam catapults are tested using weights. The arrester cables are also tested with weights. No actual aircrafts are used on the carrier until all flight deck mechanics are checked and double-checked. A crew's safety depends on the safety of its ship. The Navy does not commission a ship that has any flaws.

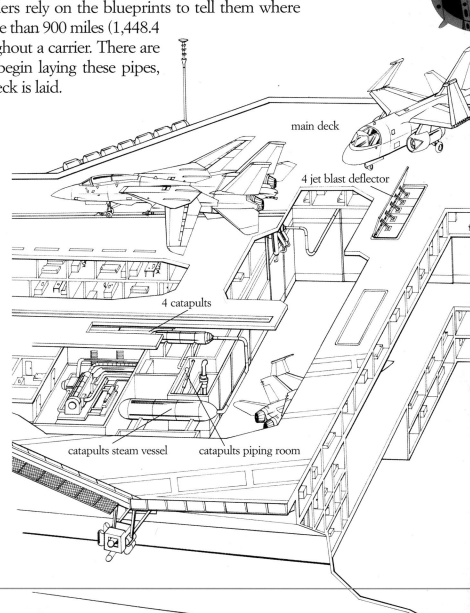

SPS-67 Surface Search Radar
SPS-49v Air Search Radar
Mk.91 Sea Sparrow SAM Illuminator
bridge
flag bridge
waterline
defrost room
engine room
main deck
4 jet blast deflector
4 catapults
catapults steam vessel
catapults piping room

primary Flight Control
squadron space
fan room
TV studios/public affairs
maintenance shops
fueling bay

command operations space

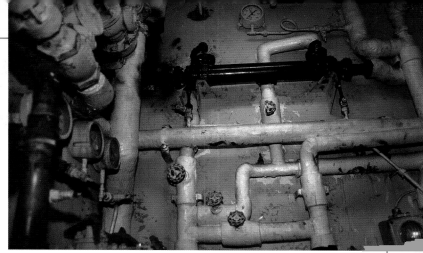

Right: Here is just one view of the more than 900 miles (1,448.4 m) of pipes, cables, and wires run throughout a carrier. This is a view from the USS *Coral Sea.*

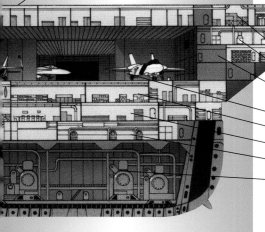

catapult equipment spaces
aviation equipment stowage
gallery (03) deck
02 deck
01 deck
main hangar deck
second deck
third deck
fourth deck
engine room

USS *Harry S. Truman*

Diagrams (top): This diagram is a cutaway view of the USS *Harry S. Truman* from the front.

Diagrams (background): This diagram is a cutaway view of the USS *Harry S. Truman* from the top.

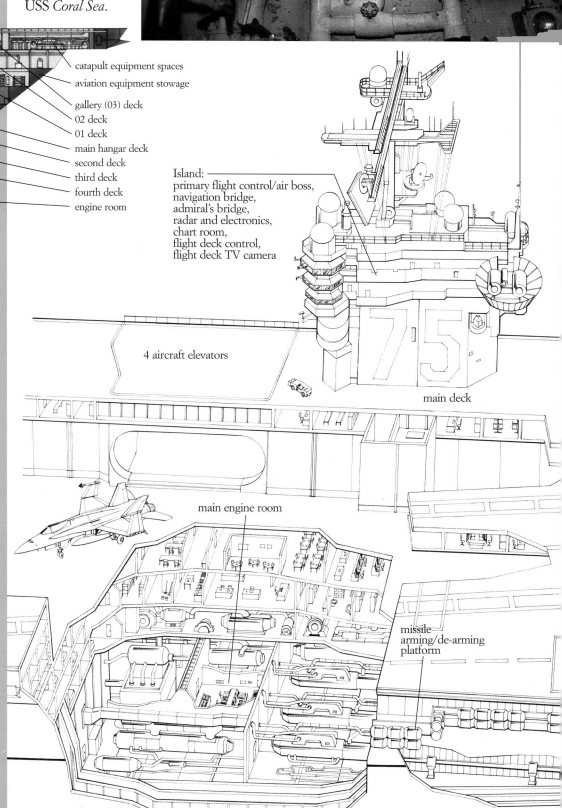

Island:
primary flight control/air boss,
navigation bridge,
admiral's bridge,
radar and electronics,
chart room,
flight deck control,
flight deck TV camera

4 aircraft elevators

main deck

main engine room

missile arming/de-arming platform

The Air Wing and Flight Operations

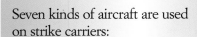

An aircraft carrier's fighting power comes from its airplane power. This is because the purpose of an aircraft carrier is to send out planes to patrol and to battle. No book about aircraft carriers is complete without talking about the ship's air wing and flight operations. An aircraft carrier has only a few dozen defensive missiles. Without its air wing, a supercarrier is a sitting duck in the water.

THE FLIGHT DECK

The most active part of any aircraft carrier is its flight deck, or as sailors call it, the "roof." All flight deck jobs focus on helping planes to take off and land. The air wing uses half the people on the ship to fly and to land more than eighty jets. That means more than three thousand sailors on the ship work only for the air wing. The other two thousand people operate the ship.

The flight deck is more than 1,000 feet (304.8 m) long and 252 feet (76.8 m) wide. The area on the flight deck is equal to 4.5 acres (1.8 ha). The work performed on the roof happens near the four elevators, the four steam catapults, and the landing area with its arrester cables.

Seven kinds of aircraft are used on strike carriers:

A-6 INTRUDER (low-level bomber)
F-14 TOMCAT (two-seat fighter)
S-3B VIKING (submarine hunter and in-air jet fuel tanker)
EA-6B PROWLER (electronic jamming plane)
F/A-18 HORNET (single-seat fighter/bomber)
E2C HAWKEYE (radar and electronics plane)
SH-60 SEAHAWK (search and rescue helicopter)

SH-60 SEAHAWK

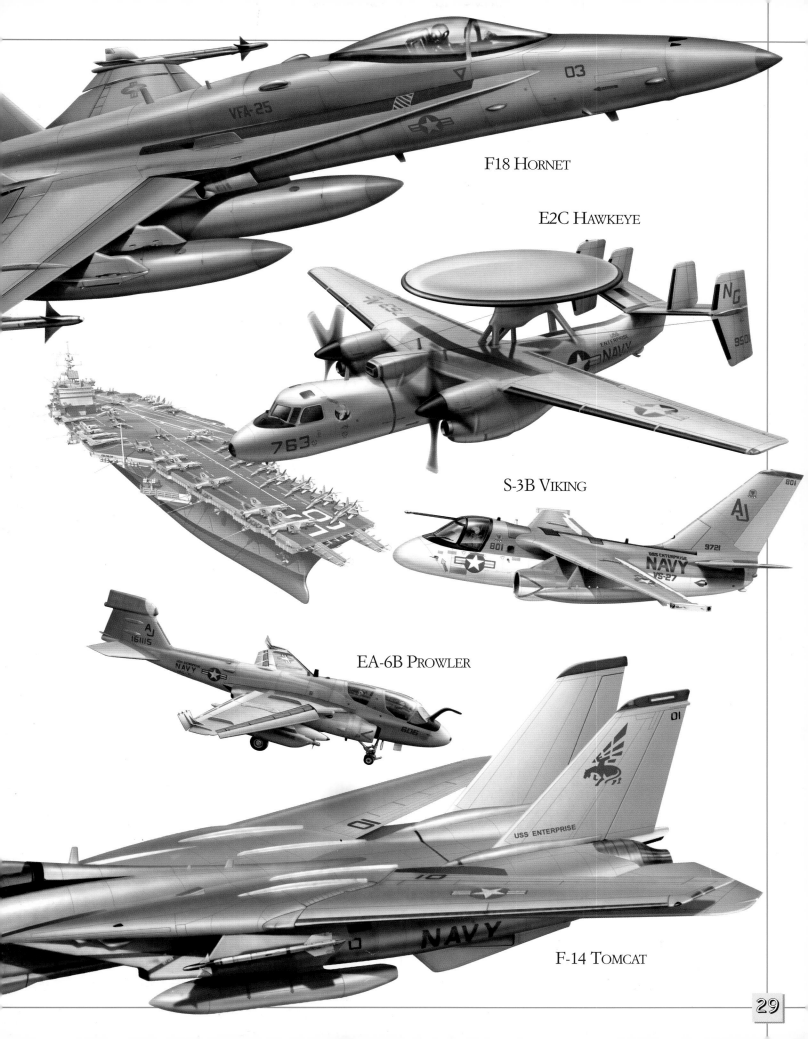

F18 Hornet

E2C Hawkeye

S-3B Viking

EA-6B Prowler

F-14 Tomcat

Elevators and the Angled Deck

Left: A Grumman F6F Hellcat fighter plane is being brought up by elevator to the flight deck of the USS *Monterey* by crewmen, in June 1944.

Below, top: A ground crew pushes an F-14 Tomcat onto an elevator at the edge of an aircraft carrier's flight deck.

Below, bottom: USS *Saratoga* plane handlers guide a Hellcat into position on the elevator to take it down to the hangar deck, in November 1943.

There are four elevators on a supercarrier. Each elevator is large enough to lift two jets with their wings folded. Two elevators are forward of the control tower on the starboard side. The other two elevators are to the rear of the control tower. One is on the right side of the ship and one is on the left side. The position of the four elevators allows smooth traffic of airplanes that are taking off and landing. When airplanes are ready for takeoff, they are loaded two at a time on one of the elevators. Once on the flight deck, they are wheeled into takeoff position and catapulted off the deck. When a plane lands, it is quickly taken to one of the rear elevators and lowered to the hangar deck.

This clears the deck for safe landings and takeoffs. The Navy does not want its planes sitting on the deck of an active carrier. If a plane were to crash during a landing, it could hit planes sitting on deck and destroy them. This kind of an accident could kill people. It could also stop carrier flight operations and hurt the battle plan.

THE ANGLED DECK
Carriers in World War II had one long flight deck. This deck ran the length of the ship. This design changed when jets came into use in the 1950s. Jets flew much faster than propeller planes. Navy experts were afraid that jets could not stop quickly enough upon landing and would crash into the planes waiting to take off on the front of the ship.

To make a carrier safer for jets, the Navy designed the angled deck on the back half of the ship. An angled deck is a shorter deck that sticks out fourteen degrees from the center of the ship. It is shorter than the front deck and ends across from the island. All aircraft land on the angled deck using arrester cables. Landing on this deck allows the pilot to take off again if the tail hook misses all the arrester cables. This keeps the forward deck safe. It also allows the forward deck to be used constantly for take off operations.

The design change actually helped carriers become more effective and powerful. The Navy realized that planes would not always be landing on the angled deck. Therefore they looked at the angled deck to see if it could be used for takeoffs, too. They discovered that the angled deck was long and wide enough to add two more steam catapults. This design helped a carrier crew quickly get more jets into the air. The angled deck was also wide enough so that a fourth elevator was added. Finally, the added weight of building the angled deck helped offset the weight of the island. Now the carrier did not have to carry extra ballast to balance the ship. All supercarriers now have angled decks and four elevators.

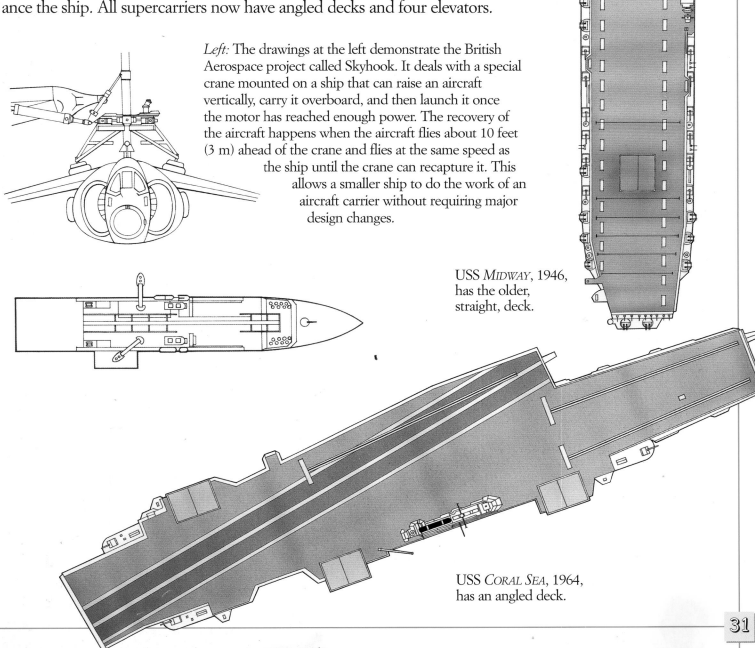

Left: The drawings at the left demonstrate the British Aerospace project called Skyhook. It deals with a special crane mounted on a ship that can raise an aircraft vertically, carry it overboard, and then launch it once the motor has reached enough power. The recovery of the aircraft happens when the aircraft flies about 10 feet (3 m) ahead of the crane and flies at the same speed as the ship until the crane can recapture it. This allows a smaller ship to do the work of an aircraft carrier without requiring major design changes.

USS *MIDWAY*, 1946, has the older, straight, deck.

USS *CORAL SEA*, 1964, has an angled deck.

Flight Operations

Jets are sent on missions almost every day that a carrier is at sea. During wartime, flight operations can continue eighteen hours a day! The air wing sailors and pilots work twelve-hour shifts. Teams of sailors have different jobs to carry out at every stage of flight operations. Each job is coordinated for people to work together. The sailors and pilots use their skills and the ship's technology to do their jobs quickly and safely.

THE FLIGHT BOSS

The flight boss controls all air wing activity. The flight boss gives orders to all hangar and flight deck crews from a room in the control tower. The deck crews load, fuel, and move planes according to the flight boss's schedule. A tabletop cutout of the flight deck helps the flight boss and his two assistants do their jobs. Models of all the airplanes sitting on the real flight deck are placed in their positions on the cutout. The assistants move the model planes as they get information from the workers on the flight deck. This cutout is about as low-tech as a job can get. When a plane takes off, the model is removed from the cutout. When a plane lands, a model is placed where the plane has stopped and then is moved as the plane is wheeled away to let another plane land.

FUEL CREWS

Fighter planes stay in the hangar until they are ready to launch. Their wings fold to make space. Loading and fueling planes takes place both in the hangar and on the flight deck. Flight deck loading and fueling is done only for planes that are flying a second mission, though. Fuel crews do all airplane fueling, using special hoses that draw fuel from tanks on the hangar deck. Fueling planes on deck is a dangerous business because it happens while flight operations move around the fueling jet. One mishap can cause a fire or, worse, an explosion.

Above and Right drawings: These drawings show the colors of the shirts worn by the people who work on an aircraft carrier. Color coding makes it easier to identify people and makes the operation of the carrier run more efficiently.

Right, photo: Even though each person has their own job, as you can see from the many different shirt colors in the photo, working on a carrier is still a team effort.

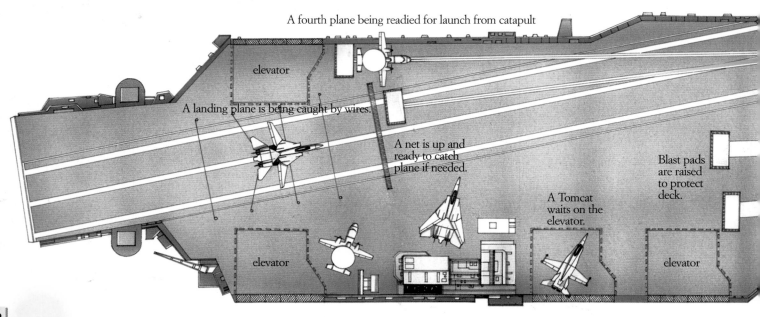

A fourth plane being readied for launch from catapult

elevator

A landing plane is being caught by wires.

A net is up and ready to catch plane if needed.

A Tomcat waits on the elevator.

Blast pads are raised to protect deck.

elevator

elevator

LOADING CREWS

Loading crews bring missiles and bombs from storage. They attach these weapons to the underside of the planes. Once the plane is loaded, it is wheeled onto an elevator by a motorized tow cart. The plane is taken up to the flight deck to wait its turn for takeoff.

Flight deck crews wear colored shirts.
Each color tells what job a person does.

YELLOW – directs airplanes into position
WHITE – safety inspectors
BROWN – maintenance
BLUE – drives tractors that pull planes
GREEN – operates catapult and arresting cables
PURPLE – fuels planes
RED – loads weapons
SILVER – performs fire and rescue operations

Below, left: This illustration shows how airplanes take off and land. At the back of the carrier a plane has caught the arresting cables. At the same time, planes are being launched by the steam catapults from the front of the carrier.

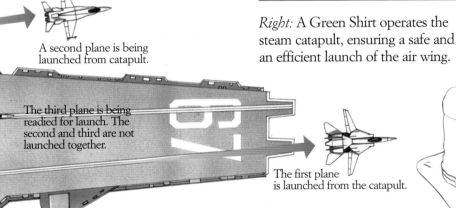

A second plane is being launched from catapult.

The third plane is being readied for launch. The second and third are not launched together.

The first plane is launched from the catapult.

Right: A Green Shirt operates the steam catapult, ensuring a safe and an efficient launch of the air wing.

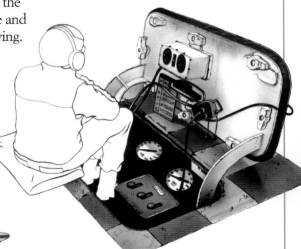

Steam Catapult

The steam catapult is one of the most complex machines on a carrier. A system of pipes sits below the surface of the flight deck. They draw steam from a generator. Valves are used to store pressurized steam in a main pipe until it is released like a gunshot. Each of the four catapults is 302 feet (92.1 m) long. A piston inside the main pipe is connected to a tow bar. Catapult crews called Green Shirts, because of the green-colored shirt they wear, attach the tow bar to an airplane's front wheels.

The pilot runs the engines up to full power and applies the brakes to keep the plane from moving forward. Full engine power is much greater than the plane's brakes can hold, however, so the plane is also connected to a steel bar, called a holdback, attached to the catapult. An engine running at full power, combined with the push given by the catapult, speeds the plane up to its best takeoff speed of 150 knots, or about 175 miles per hour (281.6 km/h).

When all systems are checked, the pilot salutes the Green Shirt outside the plane. The Green Shirt gives a "thumbs up" to the catapult officer, known as the Shooter. The Shooter sits in a compartment next to the runway. He hits a button and the steam-powered catapult shoots the plane out to sea.

The secret to a successful catapult is using the right amount of steam power. Too little power will not give the plane enough speed to take off. The plane will crash into the ocean. The right amount of steam power depends on the weight of the aircraft. Pilots know the weight of their aircraft with a full tank of fuel. They add the weight of the missiles and the bombs to the plane weight and call that down to a Green Shirt. A Green Shirt writes the airplane's weight onto a chalkboard. The Shooter looks in a book to determine the amount of steam needed to launch the aircraft based on its weight.

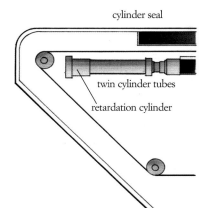

cylinder seal

twin cylinder tubes

retardation cylinder

Pilots and planes get knocked around a lot during a carrier landing. The plane drops with such force and stops so quickly that pilots call it a controlled crash.

ARRESTING CABLES

Today's high-tech jets do not fly well at low speeds because they are heavy and designed to fly best at speeds over 500 miles per hour (804.7 km/h). Therefore, jets land at 150 miles per hour (241.4 km/h)! Air brakes, or extended wing flaps, help to slow them down as they come close to the deck. The only way planes can stop on top of the ship is by catching an arresting cable with an 8-foot (2.4-m) hook let down at the tail of the plane.

ARRESTOR SYSTEM

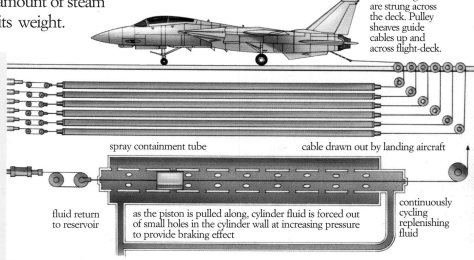

six arresting cables are strung across the deck. Pulley sheaves guide cables up and across flight-deck.

spray containment tube

cable drawn out by landing aircraft

fluid return to reservoir

as the piston is pulled along, cylinder fluid is forced out of small holes in the cylinder wall at increasing pressure to provide braking effect

continuously cycling replenishing fluid

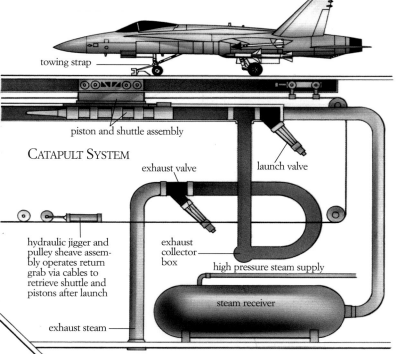

steel guide undercarriage the towing hook sticks
up from the deck

piston

group of pistons

A steam catapult has enough power
to shoot a 2,000-pound (756-kg) car more than
.5 mile (.8 km) out to sea. The catapult above allows the plane
to reach a high enough speed for take-off.

towing strap

piston and shuttle assembly

CATAPULT SYSTEM

exhaust valve

launch valve

hydraulic jigger and
pulley sheave assem-
bly operates return
grab via cables to
retrieve shuttle and
pistons after launch

exhaust
collector
box

high pressure steam supply

steam receiver

exhaust steam

Above: Catapults consist of two rows of piping in a trough
beneath the deck. A bar on the nosegear of the plane attaches
to a shuttle that sticks up above the flight deck and is connected
to pistons in the trough. There is a holdback device that keeps
the plane in place as pressure is increased. When the signal
is given, the catapult is fired. Steam floods into the cylinders
releasing the hold back and forcing the pistons, the shuttle,
and the aircraft forward. The shuttle is stopped when spears
on the pistons plunge into waterbrake cylinders.

With the help of the steam catapmult, carrier jets
can shoot from 0 to 175 miles per
hour (281.6 km/h) in less than
two seconds!

LANDING OPERATIONS

Being able to land a plane on a carrier is equally important to any air wing
mission. An aircraft carrier uses a combina-
tion of high-tech equipment and radio commu-
nication to land its planes. Pilots first contact the
Carrier Air Traffic Control Center (CATCC).
The CATCC is located in the island. A half-
dozen people use computer guidance equipment
and radar screens to follow all the planes around
the ship. The CATCC tells pilots where to fly to
set up for a landing. Often there are several
planes waiting to land at the same time. The
CATCC lines them up 4 miles (6.4 km) away
from the carrier. Under the best conditions, a jet
can land every thirty seconds.

The lens is a system of lights placed on the port
side of the ship. Pilots circle the carrier and come
in from the rear. They lower their landing gear
and the tail hook. From almost 1 mile (1.6 m)
out, a pilot can see the glowing lights of the lens,
but only when his plane is coming down at the
proper angle to land on the carrier. In the center
of the row of lights is an amber light. This is
called the Meatball. The pilot must keep the
Meatball in the center of a row of green lights. If
the plane moves too high or low, red lights
appear next to the Meatball. The Meatball
guides pilots onto the deck where their tail hooks
can catch an arresting cable.

Today's carriers use four arresting cables. The cables are
made of 2-inch (5-cm) thick braided steel. They sit
across the angled deck spaced about 50 feet (15.2 m)
apart. Each arresting cable is hooked onto a braking
system below the flight deck. The plane lands with its
tail hook down. When the plane hits the deck, the hook
grabs onto one of the cables and stops the plane within
325 feet (99.1 m). As the plane pulls at the cable, the
braking system slows the plane quickly but easily. This
braking system prevents the cable from snapping and
sending the plane into the ocean.

High-Tech Defense

You see that an aircraft carrier is only as powerful as its air wing. No carrier or air wing, however, can work without all the computers, the radar equipment, and the people who run them. Computers help sailors run almost every part of a ship. Radar gives a carrier a defensive web around it. Parts of the air wing help widen this defense. An aircraft carrier's defenses begin from the furthest points out and work inward. The carrier uses radar-carrying airplanes and Combat Air Patrol (CAP) to fight against any incoming enemy planes.

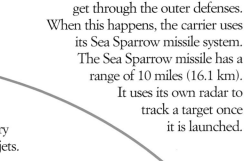

LAST LINE OF DEFENSE
A carrier's last lines of defense are its own radar and missile systems. The carrier uses radar to scan the air and sea 20 miles (32.2 km) around it. Sometimes an enemy missile or plane manages to get through the outer defenses. When this happens, the carrier uses its Sea Sparrow missile system. The Sea Sparrow missile has a range of 10 miles (16.1 km). It uses its own radar to track a target once it is launched.

SH-60 Sea Hawks are sub-seeking helicopters. They fly away from the ship and drop sonar buoys into the water. The sonar sound waves seek enemy sub positions. Once found, Seahawks send the sub's position to Viking jets.

F-14 Tomcat jets protect carriers against enemy aircraft that come close to the carrier. Tomcats carry their own radar to find enemy jets. They have missiles that can destroy enemy targets 20 miles (32.2 km) away.

EA-6 Prowler jets use radar-jamming equipment to interrupt enemy radar. Radar-jamming equipment sends out electronic signals that prevent enemy missiles and planes from finding a carrier.

information

information

20 miles (32.2 km)

150 miles (241.4 km)

last defense

S-3B Viking jets hunt for enemy submarines. Viking jets use special radar and infrared, or heat-finding seekers to find submarines, or subs, below the water. Once found, Vikings drop torpedoes to attack the submarines.

Supercarriers have a defense that reaches about 150 miles (241.4 km) outward. This defense begins with Airborne Early Warning (AEW) aircraft. This plane is loaded with radar and electronic equipment. It serves as the carrier's eyes and ears.

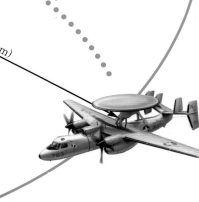

first defense

RADAR TRACKING
Radar uses radio waves to track objects in the air or on the ground. Radar units shoot radio waves into the air. These radio waves bounce off anything in the air or on the ground. The bouncing waves return to the radar units and show an image on a video screen.

BIG
E

655

BEWARE OF JET
BLASTPROPS
AND ROTORS

The Island is the center of flight operations on a carrier. The top level is the Control Tower that directs all aircraft movement on the flight deck and within 5 miles (8 km) of the carrier. The Navigational Bridge is the next level where the movement of the ship itself is directed. The next level is the Flag Bridge which would be used by an admiral and his staff were he or she on board the carrier.

Light Carriers

Some aircraft carriers are smaller and lighter than the Nimitz-class supercarriers. These lighter carriers cost a lot less money to build. Each performs special duties for the navy that uses them.

Most foreign navies use these smaller and lighter carriers because of their lower cost compared to a supercarrier. There are forty aircraft carriers in the world. The U.S. Navy uses twenty-four carriers: twelve of these are supercarriers and twelve are light carriers. Russia has one supercarrier left from its former powerhouse navy; four other small carriers have been taken out of service. Britain has five light carriers. India has two small carriers, which they bought from the British. France has two light carriers, and Italy and Spain each have one light carrier.

The technology for all these carriers comes mostly from the United States, which is the world leader in military technology. Its designs and weapon systems have been sold to friendly countries or copied by those countries' own naval engineers. Some carrier design changes, though, have come from other navies, such as the ski ramp used by the British navy.

INVINCIBLE
This drawing shows the double launcher for *Invincible's* Sea Dart air-surface missiles.

HMS *INVINCIBLE*

INVINCIBLE-CLASS CARRIERS

The British navy built its Invincible-class carriers for antisubmarine duties. They store Sea King helicopters and Harrier jump jets in their hangars. They carry up to ten helicopters and fourteen jump jets.

Invincible-class carriers are almost half the size of Nimitz-class attack carriers. They are built smaller because helicopters and jump jets don't need a lot of space to take off. Invincible-class carriers steam up to 32 miles per hour (51.5 km/h) and have their own air defenses. They also repair aircraft below decks allowing the ship to remain at sea for many months.

The Invincible-class carriers also have a runway. This runway is short, but has a ski ramp at the end of the bow to give a plane extra lift on takeoff. The ski ramp design is simple and saves the cost and maintenance needed for catapult systems. When a plane shoots down the runway, it hits the ski ramp and sends itself up into the air. This helps the plane gain altitude quickly. Lighter jets, like the Harrier, use the ski ramps when they are needed to carry extra fuel or missiles. A vertical takeoff uses too much fuel with this extra weight.

HOW JUMP JETS WORK

The jump jet uses a Vertical Takeoff and Landing (VTOL) system. Its jet engines turn downward to lift the plane off the ground. While in the air, the engines rotate to give the jet forward speed. When the jet reaches 170 miles per hour (273.6 km/h), it begins to fly like a regular plane.

The Harrier jump jet is the main defense for antisubmarine carriers. The Harrier is a fighter plane able to shoot at ground and air targets from a range of 25 miles (40.2 km). The jump jet is a special aircraft because it can take off and land with no forward roll, moving straight up and down like a helicopter. This makes the Harrier a perfect defense airplane for a small aircraft carrier.

ANTISUBMARINE HELICOPTERS

The Sea King helicopters are used to hunt submarines. Two helicopters take off from the top deck and patrol the sea around the ship. The first Sea King drops a sonar buoy into the water. The sonar picks up the sound from the sub's propeller. The second Sea King drops a Stingray homing torpedo into the water. The homing torpedo uses its own sonar to find and to destroy the sub.

Carriers Around the World

RUSSIAN AIRCRAFT CARRIERS

Russia's aircraft carrier program got off to a late start, with their first carrier commissioned in 1965. The ships were unable to provide enough coverage to be useful in naval operations. Therefore, the Russians looked to U.S. designs to inform their later attempts at building a strong aircraft carrier and air wing. Unfortunately, many political and budget cuts made it difficult for the navy to get construction off the ground. They needed to compromise. The Kiev-class ships were the compromise. This class of ships worked well but were never itended for permanent use. Finally a midsized, ski-jump carrier was commissioned in 1991. The ship's name is *Admiral Kuznetsov* and it is the only aircraft carrier remaining in the Russian navy.

THE FRENCH NUCLEAR-POWERED CARRIER

The French commissioned the *Charles de Gaulle* in 2000. This is their first nuclear-powered aircraft, designed to replace the conventionally-powered *Clemenceau*. The new ship is 40 percent larger than *Clemenceau*. *Charles de Gaulle* has three arresting cables, and catapults that can launch one aircraft per minute. The carrier uses two nuclear pressure water reactors and has the capacity to run at 25 knots continuously for five years before refueling. France plans to build another carrier in the *Charles de Gaulle* class to remain the most powerful navy in Europe.

Right: These overhead views of the various light carriers show the basic shapes used by the navies around the world.

CLEMENCEAU
This is a turret for a 100mm automatic cannon on *Clemenceau*

CLEMENCEAU

ITALIAN CRUISER CARRIER

The Italians use mainly light, or cruiser, carriers in their navy. In the past, these carriers carried mainly helicopters, or craft that could take off and land vertically. Their newest cruiser, named *Giuseppe Garibaldi*, was designed to be able to carry fixed wing aircraft as well as helicopters. This means the carrier takes on a new role in the Italian navy. Rather than focusing primarily on Anti-submarine Warfare (ASW), the carrier now serves much like the U.S. supercarriers. It is meant to provide air superiority in the area of operations of the naval fleet, and to operate as the advance defense in any naval situation. It has been designed to be as flexible as possible in terms of the types of aircraft that can be carried, depending on the need during a particular naval operation.

GARIBALDI
Garibaldi has launchers with two groups of four cells, for the Albatross system, that launch two Aspide missiles similar to those on the Sparrow.

GIUSEPPE GARIBALDI

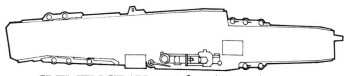

CLEMENCEAU 876 feet (267 m)

PRINCIPE DE ASTURIAS 643 feet (196 m)

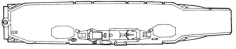

GARIBALDI 591 feet (180 m)

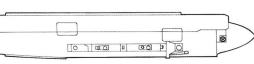

INVINCIBLE 676 feet (206 m)

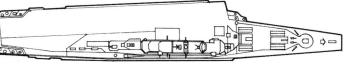

KIEV 899 feet (274 m)

The HMS *Invincible's* ski jump deck provides extra lift, allowing the British air wing to launch quickly without needing too much room to gather speed.

KIEV

THE *KIEV'S* ELECTRONIC COUNTERMEASURES (ECM)

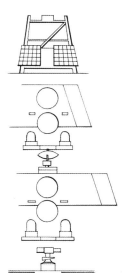

Rum Tub is NATO's nickname for the naval ESM used by Russia on its carriers. Naval ESMs and ECMs are used to detect enemy radar or other threats.

Strut Pair radar antenna look for aircraft.

Bell Bash is another Russian ECM antenna.

Palm Frond is the name for the navigational radar used on *Kiev.*

Bell Thump ECM antenna is another method to detect and work against enemy attacks.

Bell Crown is an electro-optical antenna.

KIEV
This is one of *Kiev's* Gatling 30 mm machine guns.

The Future of Aircraft Carriers

How much better and powerful can aircraft carriers become? That's a hard question to answer. Aircraft carriers cannot be built much larger than they are today, and they will always be able to carry only a certain number of aircraft. Each battle needs enough firepower, but no more than is needed. That means increased size really isn't the answer. The future of aircraft carriers lies in better naval and airplane technology.

STEALTH SHIP

The stealth bomber and stealth fighter have been used for more than ten years. Each plane uses a special shape and antiradar technology to fly without being detected. Navy experts are now looking at how stealth technology can be used for ships. Radar easily spots ships today. Ships are huge and bulky. They have up to four propellers that make a lot of noise under water. How can you hide from radar a ship the size of an office building? Well, you can't hide it completely, but you can make it seem to enemy radar as though it is smaller than its actual size. This is the kind of technology that the U.S. Navy is now testing.

Some experts say that decreasing the height and the size of a carrier's control tower will help in making the ship look smaller on radar screens. Using radar-absorbing materials to build the ship will decrease its apparent size even more. An enemy will then think the ship is a destroyer or another smaller ship. This gives a great advantage to the carrier because it will have the element of surprise against an enemy. Making a carrier shrink under radar's electronic eyes is not the only improvement needed for the future.

In the future, stealth bombers and other stealth aircraft can be flown off an aircraft carrier. Take a look at this illustration of the stealth bomber. Can you imagine what a stealth aircraft carrier would look like?

AUTOMATION

The U.S. Navy is testing systems that can work without the help of humans. Automated, or Smart Ship technology, will cut costs. Fewer sailors on a ship means less money spent and fewer lives lost during battle operations. Computerized radar systems cut the need for so many radar operators, and automated weapon loading systems can cut the need for so many human weapons loaders. Which systems will be fully automated is yet unknown, but the two most likely are computerized radar systems and automated weapons loading systems. Eventually, the Navy also hopes to use unmanned aircraft in battles. These planes, or Unmanned Combat Aerial Vehicles (UCAV), will help reduce the number of humans flying warplanes. The UCAV is a remote-controlled fighter and bomber that will use ground and air-based computers to help it locate targets. Once a target is destroyed, the UCAV can be flown back to a carrier. UCAVs will make combat cheaper, saving both money and lives.

SPECIAL MISSIONS

Future aircraft carriers will be able to do more than ferry planes around the world. Carriers will be outfitted to help with disasters around the world as well. They will carry supplies or will be used as hospitals. They can also be used to transport troops. Designers are now changing how the inside of a carrier can be used. The hangar decks will be redesigned so that they can quickly be changed into hospital rooms. Weapons storage areas will be designed so they can be quickly changed into troop transport sleeping areas. A carrier that can be used for many different tasks other than battle is a money and life-saving ship for any navy.

Airplane hangars are also being redesigned. In the future they must be able to store new types of aircraft. Tilt-wing planes, vertical takeoff aircraft, and unmanned aircraft will be the future of naval aviation.

THE CHANGING FACE OF CARRIERS

The future of the aircraft carrier depends on change and innovation. The United States is the leader in naval power and electronic design. Designers are always at work keeping the navy ahead of possible enemies. The goal is to build better but fewer carriers that use fewer people to operate them. Such innovation will save lives and money, while keeping the world safe from warring nations.

Glossary

air wing (AYR WING) The planes used on an aircraft carrier.

angled deck (AN-guld DEK) A second deck on a carrier angled fourteen degrees from the center.

antiradar technology (AN-tie-RAY-dar tek-NAH-luh-jee) A "stealth" science that uses shape and special materials to make a vehicle invisible to radar.

arrester cables (a-RES-ter KAY-buls) Thick steel wires used to help stop landing planes.

attack carriers (uh-TAK KAR-ee-urz) Aircraft carriers using fighter aircraft as their main weapons.

blueprints (BLOO-prints) Paper plans that have printed designs to build something.

Bridge (BRIJ) The area on a ship from where the captain commands the boat.

Carrier Air Traffic Control Center (CATCC) (KAR-ee-ur AYR TRA-fik kun-TROHL SEN-ter) The room in the carrier from which radar operators direct airplanes near the carrier.

catapult (KA-tuh-pult) A machine that pushes a plane along a runway to help it gain speed for take off.

commissioned (ka-MIH-shund) To put into service.

Computer Aided Design (kum-PYOO-ter AY-ded dih-ZYN) A computer program that helps engineers draw up plans to make machines.

defensive missile system (dih-FEN-siv MIH-sul SIS-tum) A system of missiles used to shoot down attacking enemy planes.

designs (dih-ZYNZ) Preliminary sketch or outline showing the main features of something to be built or created; plans on how to build something.

draft (DRAFT) How deep a boat sits in the water.

dry dock (DRIE DOK) A boat dock that keeps out water until the boat can be built strong enough to float.

flight boss (FLYT BOS) A naval officer who directs airplanes and crew on the flight deck.

flight deck (FLYT DEK) The top deck of an aircraft carrier where planes land and take off.

forward presence (FOR-wurd PREH-zints) A term used to describe how a carrier uses its power close to a battle.

frames (FRAYMS) Sections of a carrier that are numbered so sailors can find their way through the passages.

hangars (HANG-ers) Places where planes are stored.

helicopter carriers (HEH-luh-kop-ter KAR-ee-urs) Smaller aircraft carriers that carry only helicopters into a battle area.

hulls (HULZ) The bodies of ships.

keel (KEEL) The bottom of a ship that runs from front to back.

lens (LENZ) A system of lights used by pilots to line up their planes for a safe carrier landing.

light carriers (LITE KAR-ee-urs) Small aircraft

carriers that have a smaller number of planes in their air wing.

Meatball (MEET-bol) An amber-colored light on the lens landing system that tells a pilot the plane is in the right position to land.

Nimitz-class (NIM-itz-KLAS) The name for the largest type of aircraft carriers.

nuclear reactors (NOO-clee-ur ree-AK-turs) An energy system using atomic power to drive engines.

propellers (pruh-PEH-lurs) Metal shafts with blades that move a ship when turned.

sea trials (SEE TRY-uls) Tests that navy ships go through to make sure all parts and systems of a ship run properly.

technology (tek-NAH-luh-jee) The building and use of machines.

turbines (TER-bynz) A motor that turns by water, air, or steam.

Vertical Takeoff and Landing (VTOL) (VER-tih-cul TAY-koff and LAN-ding) A jet system that uses rotating engines to lift a plane off the ground and move it forward until it flies like an airplane.

Additional Resources

For additional information on aircraft carriers, check out the following books, videos, and Web sites.

Books
Buyan, Michael. *Supercarriers (Land and Sea)*. Capstone Press: Mankato, MN, 2001.
Pelta, Kathy. *The U.S. Navy*. Learner Publications: Minneapolis, MN, 1990.
Peston, Anthony. *The World's Greatest Aircraft Carriers: From Civil War to Present*.
Thunder Bay Press: San Diego, CA, 2000.

Video tapes
The Big Aircraft Carrier. VanDerKloot Film & Television. Little Mammoth Media.
Carrier: Fortress at Sea. Discovery Channel.
City of Steel: Carrier. Discovery Channel.

Web Sites
www.bluejacket.com/usn_aircraft_carriers.htm
www.chinfo.navy.mil/navpalib/carriers

Index

R

S

T

U

W

Z

About the Author

Mark Beyer has written more than fifty young adult and children's books. Writing on history and technology are two of his favorite subjects. He has recently written another book on aircraft carriers for a first-grade audience. Mark lives with his wife, Lucy, in a farm cottage outside New York City.

Photo Credits